Sister Wisdom

INSIGHTS *from* GREAT WOMEN

This was only the beginning.

Sister Wisdom

©2004 Elm Hill Books, an imprint of J. Countryman®, a division of Thomas Nelson, Inc.
Nashville, TN 37214

The quoted ideas expressed in this book (but not scripture verses) are not, in all cases, exact quotations, as some have been edited for clarity and brevity. In all cases, the author has attempted to maintain the speaker's original intent. In some cases, quoted material for this book was obtained from secondary sources, primarily print media. While every effort was made to ensure the accuracy of these sources, the accuracy cannot be guaranteed. For additions, deletions, corrections or clarifications in future editions of this text, please write ELM HILL BOOKS.

Cover Design and Page Layout: Margaret Pesek

ISBN 1-4041-8558-5 *(softcover)*
       1-4041-8537-2 *(hardcover)*

CRISWELL FREEMAN

—〰—

The Washington Post called Criswell Freeman "possibly the most prolific 'quote book' writer in America." With little fanfare, Dr. Freeman has compiled and edited well over a hundred titles that have now sold over 8,000,000 copies. Criswell is a Doctor of Clinical Psychology, earning his undergraduate degree at Vanderbilt University. He is married and has two daughters.

ANTOINETTE HARGROVE

—〰—

Antoinette Hargrove earned her B.S. from Athens State College in Alabama, and a Masters of Science in Organizational Leadership from Cumberland University (Lebanon, TN). She strives to uphold spiritual values and also provide character-building lessons through sisterly and brotherly love. In addition to public speaking, she ministers to various churches during annual Women's Day events, and volunteers her services for charitable organizations that seek to minister to children and the elderly.

Sister Wisdom

Table of Contents

INTRODUCTION

—⚋⚋—

Women of color truly found their collective voice in the 20th century. Prior to that time, only a few courageous pioneers were able to fight their way into the national spotlight. Although slavery in America was abolished by the Emancipation Proclamation in 1863, institutionalized segregation—combined with almost universal prejudice— limited opportunities for African-Americans. Then, almost a full century after Lincoln signed into law the proclamation that ended slavery, things began to change.

A pivotal moment came on December 1, 1955, when a 42-year-old African-American woman named Rosa Parks boarded a bus in Montgomery, Alabama. When ordered to give up her seat to a white woman, Parks refused and was arrested. Her actions unwittingly gained national coverage of the injustices in race relations, her courage helped to energize the civil rights movement in America, and Rosa Parks became a national icon. Although she made a daring and determined decision that day, she could have never imagined the impact her decision would have on the movement toward equality for African-Americans and women. *This was only the beginning.*

Chapter 1
LIFE
PEARL BAILEY

—ᴧᴧ—

I never looked for things. I just watched for the way the
Good Lord turned my feet, and that's the direction I went.

—*Pearl Bailey*

Although she was never formally trained in music, Pearl Bailey crafted a musical career that lasted six decades and touched the hearts of millions. Having learned to sing in the church where her father preached, Pearl began her professional singing career in the era of big bands. Eventually, she became a star on stage and on screen, including her best-known role as the lead in *Hello Dolly!*

At the age of 67, Pearl graduated from Georgetown University. She also honored her country by serving as a special ambassador to the United Nations.

As a capstone to her many accomplishments, Miss Bailey received a Presidential Medal of Freedom in 1988. Two years later, as Americans mourned her death, a grateful nation looked back on the life of a talented woman who always shared her talents, her wisdom, and her love. May each of us, in our own ways, follow her example by striving for the best in our lives and encouraging others to seek the best in theirs.

Look at me. I am black. I am beautiful.

—*Mary McLeod Bethune*

*God's hand must have closed over me very early
in life, making me tough and headstrong and
resilient. It is His hand that carried me safely down
the long, dark, road I've had to follow since.*

—*Ethel Waters*

Life is accepting what is and working from that.

—*Gloria Naylor*

THE MORE YOU PRAISE
AND CELEBRATE YOUR LIFE,
THE MORE THERE IS
IN LIFE TO CELEBRATE.

—Oprah Winfrey

*Life loves to be taken by the lapel and told,
"I am with you kid. Let's go."*

—Maya Angelou

*Life is a journey; every experience is here to teach
you more fully how to be who you really are.*

—Oprah Winfrey

*There are years that ask questions and years
that answer.*

—Zora Neale Hurston

Glorify things of the spirit and keep the things of the flesh under control.

—*Nannie Burroughs*

If we accept that Life is a gift, it seems to me we must then accept the notion that we ought to do something with this gift.

—*Dorothy Cotton*

17

At certain times I have no race. I am me. I belong to no race or time. I am the eternal feminine with its string of beads.

—Zora Neale Hurston

Revolution begins with the self, in the self.

—Toni Cade Bambara

The great I AM of the world took the soul of the world and wrapped some flesh around it and that made you.

—*Zora Neale Hurston*

My recipe for life is not being afraid of myself.

—*Eartha Kitt*

Each of us doesn't have to reinvent the world.
You don't have to try to do everything yourself.
You can learn just as much by watching and
listening as by doing.

—*Bessie Delaney*

The quality of light by which we scrutinize our
lives has direct bearing upon the product which we
live, and upon the changes which we hope to bring
about through those lives.

—*Audre Lorde*

If you want to be respected for your actions, then
your behavior must be above reproach.

—*Rosa Parks*

Living life as art requires a readiness to forgive.

—Maya Angelou

You cannot belong to anyone else until you belong to yourself.

—Pearl Bailey

What we need are mental and spiritual giants who are aflame with a purpose. We're a people ready for crusade, for we've recognized that we must work for our own salvation.

—Nannie Burroughs

I will never give in to old age until I become old. And I'm not old yet!

—*Tina Turner*

We have slumbered and slept too long already; the day is far spent; the night of death approaches.

—*Maria W. Stewart*

I am not going to die; I'm going home like a shooting star.

—*Sojourner Truth*

Chapter 2
FAITH AND DETERMINATION
SUSAN L. TAYLOR

—⁂—

Seeds of faith are always within us; sometimes it takes a crisis to nourish and encourage their growth.

—Susan L. Taylor

A fourth-generation entrepreneur, Susan L. Taylor is the editorial director of *Essence* magazine, the most highly regarded magazine for African-American women in the world. Through determination and dedication, she has guided *Essence* through phenomenal growth, launched her own line of cosmetics, functions as the executive producer of the nationally televised "Essence Awards," and has received many honors for her varied and vast accomplishments.

Mrs. Taylor is able to inspire millions of people through *Essence,* her faith-based writing, public appearances, and her monthly column, "In the Spirit," which promotes the positive aspects of the African-American community.

An avid supporter of several organizations, Mrs. Taylor is personally comitted to serving and empowering the poor and working with disadvantaged teenagers and women to enable them to attain their dreams, realize their strengths, and take charge of their lives. She has become a very visable role-model for women, encouraging them to excel, achieve, and take charge of their own directions in life.

Faith ought not to be a plaything. If we believe, we should believe like giants.

—Mary McLeod Bethune

Determination and perseverance moved the world; thinking that others will do it for you is a sure way to fail.

—Marva Collins

Little becomes much as you place it in the Master's hand.

—Dorothy Cotton

There isn't a certain time that we should set aside to talk about God. God is part of our every waking moment.

—Marva Collins

Prayer begins where human capacity ends.

—Marian Anderson

No matter how far a person can go, the horizon is still way beyond you.

—Zora Neale Hurston

I pray hard, work hard, and leave the rest to God.

—Florence Griffith Joyner

It's too big for us to be mere people.
We've got to give up being people and feel like
the tools of destiny; that's a big honor in itself.

—*Zora Neale Hurston*

Something said within my breast, "Press forward,
I will be with thee." And my heart made this
reply, "Lord, if thou wilt be with me, then I will
speak for thee as long as I live."

—*Maria W. Stewart*

There's probably little in life that matters more than first believing in one's ability to do something, and then having the sheer grit, the sheer determination, the perseverance to carry it through.

—Johnetta B. Cole

Success is within your grasp.
If you believe it is possible, you can make it happen.

—Beatryce Nivens

Ask for what you want and be prepared to get it.

—Maya Angelou

FAITH IN GOD IS
THE GREATEST POWER...
BUT GREAT, TOO, IS
FAITH IN ONESELF.

—Mary McLeod Bethune

Come up from the lowlands; there are heights yet
to climb. You cannot do healthful thinking
in the lowlands. Look to the mountaintop for faith.

—*Mary McLeod Bethune*

Nothing is easy to the unwilling.

—*Nikki Giovanni*

Faith is tested many times a day.

—Maya Angelou

Without faith, nothing is possible. With it, nothing is impossible.

—Mary McLeod Bethune

Chapter 3
USING GOD'S GIFTS
MARIAN ANDERSON

—\m—

God gives everyone a gift; everyone has a talent for something.

—*Marian Anderson*

In 1939, faculty members from Howard University attempted to arrange a concert at Constitution Hall; the concert was intended to feature the immensely gifted Marian Anderson, arguably the most talented operatic singer of her generation. But the owners of Constitution Hall, the Daughters of the American Revolution, flatly refused to allow Anderson to perform because of the color of her skin.

In response, First Lady Eleanor Roosevelt actively encouraged a plan to allow Anderson to perform on the steps of the Lincoln Memorial. And so, on Easter Sunday, April 9, 1939, Marian Anderson proudly sang before an audience that consisted of 75,000 attendees and millions of radio listeners. Her concert, and the attendant news coverage of the event, brought attention to the discrimination and the prejudice that permeated the very fabric of American life.

Marian Anderson was a woman whose towering talent was large enough to tower over the racism of her time. In the face of adversity, she nurtured the gifts God gave her, and she used those gifts to make the world a better place.

Tremendous amounts of talent are being lost to our society just because that talent wears a skirt.

—Shirley Chisholm

Challenges make you discover things about yourself that you never really knew.

—Cicely Tyson

You can't copy anybody and end up with anything. If you copy, it means you're working without any real feeling. And without feeling, whatever you do amounts to nothing.

—Billie Holiday

Each human is uniquely different. Like snowflakes, the human pattern is never cast twice.

—Alice Childress

WHEN YOU FIND
YOUR PASSION, NOT JUST
WHAT YOU LIKE TO DO
BUT THAT WHICH
MAKES YOU WANT TO
GET UP EVERY MORNING,
YOU TOO WILL
HAVE A LIFE-CHANGING
EXPERIENCE.

—*Condoleezza Rice*

*Human beings are equipped with divinely
planted yearnings and longings. That's what the
Constitution means by "certain inalienable rights."*

—Nannie Burroughs

*Always continue the climb. It is possible for you to
do whatever you choose if you first get to know who
you are, and if you are willing to work with a
power that is greater than ourselves to do it.*

—Oprah Winfrey

*Most of us who aspire to be tops in our fields
don't really consider the amount of work required
to stay on top.*

—Althea Gibson

I never intended to become a run-of-the-mill person.

—Barbara Jordan

I would strongly recommend to you to improve your talents; let not one lie buried in the earth.

—Maria W. Stewart

I didn't think of myself as gifted. I just know I had things to do. You don't think of it as being gifted when you're Black and you're poor. You think of it as moving on.

—Roberta Flack

SUCH AS I AM,

I AM A PRECIOUS GIFT.

—Zora Neale Hurston

There's a time in life when we swallow a knowledge of ourselves, and it becomes either good or sour inside.

—Pearl Bailey

There is no obstacle in the path of young people who are poor or members of minority groups that hard work and preparation cannot cure.

—Barbara Jordan

It is easy to excel at what you are good at. So, work hard and explore your talents.

—Tonya Bolden

*Once you understand what your work is and you
do not try to avert your eyes from it, but attempt to
invest energy in getting that work done, the universe
will send you what you need.*

—*Toni Cade Bambara*

No one can figure out your worth but you.

—*Pearl Bailey*

*The challenge facing us is to equip ourselves.
Then, we will be able to take our place wherever
we are in the affairs of men.*

—*Barbara Jordan*

Chapter 4
GIVING OUR BEST
ALTHEA GIBSON

—ɯ—

I pray, but I don't pray to win. I pray for the inspiration to give my best.

—Althea Gibson

She was, without a doubt, an extremely gifted tennis player. But in the 1950s, it wasn't easy for an African-American to get a break—on court or off. And as a young black girl from South Carolina, the odds against her winning a Wimbledon Championship were quite literally a million to one, if not more. But those long odds didn't deter Althea Gibson; instead, those odds fed her deep-rooted determination to be the best.

In an era when black Americans weren't even allowed to play on most tennis courts, Gibson fashioned herself into a champion. She practiced whenever she could find a court. And when Althea was finally allowed to play, she was ready. She won the French Open, the U.S. Open, and Wimbledon.

Althea Gibson's life reminds us that failure is always the path of least persistence. So if you're facing long odds, remember the story of a young girl without a court to play on, who gave her best and passed the test.

EXCELLENCE IS NOT
AN ACT BUT A HABIT.
THE THINGS YOU DO
the MOST ARE the THINGS
YOU WILL DO BEST.

—*Marva Collins*

Sometimes you have to give a little to get a lot.

—*Shirley Chisholm*

People think I'm temperamental because I know what I want.

—*Anita Baker*

Don't feel entitled to anything you didn't sweat and struggle for.

—*Marian Wright Edelman*

I train myself for triumph by knowing it is mine no matter what.

—*Audre Lorde*

SOME PEOPLE
SAY I'M FEISTY. SOME SAY
I'M TOUGH. COMBATIVE.
IN THE COMMUNITY
WHERE I COME FROM—
THE COMMUNITY
OF SURVIVAL—THOSE
WERE CONSIDERED
GOOD QUALITIES.

—Maxine Waters

Tell our children they're not going to jive their way up the career ladder. They have to work their way up hard. There's no fast elevator to the top.

—Marian Wright Edelman

The first and worst of all frauds is to cheat one's self. All sin is easy after that.

—Pearl Bailey

*Teach the children pride. Nothing learned
is worth anything if you don't know how to be
proud of yourself.*

—Nannie Burroughs

*My mother taught me very early to believe that
I could achieve any accomplishment I wanted to.
The first was to walk without braces.*

—Wilma Rudolph

*Doing the best at this moment puts you in the best
place for the next moment.*

—Oprah Winfrey

A man without ambition is dead.
A man with ambition but no love is dead.
A man with ambition and love for his blessings
here on earth is ever so alive.

—*Pearl Bailey*

From the first, I made my learning, what little it
was, useful in every way that I could.

—*Mary McLeod Bethune*

*My mother was instrumental in making
me believe that you can accomplish anything if you
believe in it.*

—Wilma Rudolph

Whoever said anybody has a right to give up?

—Marian Wright Edelman

*I say if it's going to be done, let's do it. Let's not
put it in the hands of fate. Let's take a deep breath
and go ahead.*

—Anita Baker

Just don't give up trying to do what you really want to do. Where there is love and inspiration, I don't think you can go wrong.

—Ella Fitzgerald

Nothing is going to be handed to you. You have to make things happen.

—Florence Griffith Joyner

Exhaust the little moment. Soon it dies.

—Gwendolyn Brooks

If we can recognize when something's not right, we can get the help we need. Only when we take care of ourselves, inside and out, can we be at our best.

—Julia Boyd

It is time we rolled up our sleeves and put ourselves at the top of our commitment list.

—Marian Wright Edelman

We must exchange the philosophy of excuse—what I am is beyond my control—for the philosophy of personal responsibility.

—Barbara Jordan

To do less than your best is a sin.

—Oprah Winfrey

IT DOESN'T MATTER WHAT
YOU'RE TRYING TO
ACCOMPLISH. IT'S ALL A
MATTER OF DISCIPLINE

—Wilma Rudolph

Chapter 5
COURAGE
ROSA PARKS
—◊◊◊—

God did away with all my fear. It was time for someone to stand up—or in my case, sit down. So I refused to move.

—Rosa Parks

The year was 1955, and she was riding a bus in Montgomery, Alabama. In those days, African-Americans were required to go give up their seats to whites. But she refused—so she was arrested. Her name was Rosa Parks, and her personal protest against injustice ignited the civil rights movement in America. Ms. Parks' philosophy was powerfully simple. She said, "I don't waste too much time thinking about my problems. I just look around to see what I can do, and then I do it." Difficult times call for courageous measures and this certainly was a courageous move.

Running away from problems only perpetuates them; fear begets more fear, and anxiety is a poor counselor. So if you think that you can't make changes in your world, think again. And while you're at it, remember a former seamstress named Rosa Parks. Then, after you've remembered her sacrifice, become inspired. Summon the courage to make big changes in your own life and in your world. Reach out to others and inspire them. Rosa did it, and so can you.

IF ROSA PARKS HAD
TAKEN A POLL BEFORE
SHE SAT DOWN IN THE BUS
IN MONTGOMERY, SHE'D
STILL BE STANDING.

—*Mary Frances Berry*

...I FIGURED WE NEEDED
HELP TO GET US
MORE JOBS AND
BETTER EDUCATION...
I MADE UP MY MIND
NOT TO MOVE.

—Rosa Parks

You have to be taught to be second class; you're not born that way.

—Lena Horne

The legacy of courage left by heroic black women was amassed, deed by deed, day by day, without praise or encouragement.

—Johnetta B. Cole

If we have the courage and tenacity of our forebears, who stood firmly like a rock against the lash of slavery, we shall find a way to do for our day what they did for theirs.

—Mary McLeod Bethune

When I dare to be powerful—to use my strength in the service of my vision—then it becomes less and important whether I am afraid.

—Audre Lorde

I have a lot of things to prove to myself. One is that I can live my life fearlessly.

—Oprah Winfrey

I'm a fighter; nobody has ever bought me or bossed me.

—Shirley Chisholm

I will stand my ground. Somebody must die in this cause. I may be doomed to the stake and the fire or to the scaffold tree, but it is not for me to falter.

—Sojourner Truth

One isn't necessarily born with courage, but one is born with potential. Without courage, we cannot practice any other virtue with consistency. We can't be kind, true, merciful, generous, or honest.

—*Maya Angelou*

Haven't all great leaders had grand ideas, and haven't they held fast to them in the face of attack?

—*Dorothy Cotton*

We could lose. But we couldn't not fight.

—*Audre Lorde*

I have learned over the years that when one's mind is made up this diminishes fear; knowing what must be done does away with fear.

—*Rosa Parks*

Ours is the truest dignity of man: the dignity of the undefeated.

—*Ethel Waters*

Non-violence is a way of life for courageous people.

—*Dorothy Cotton*

Anything that is as old as racism is in the bloodline of the nation. It's not any superficial thing—that attitude is in the blood, and we have to educate it out.

—Nannie Burroughs

The civil rights movement that rearranged the social order of this country did not emanate from the halls of the Harvards and Princetons and Cornells. It came from the simple unlettered people who learned that they had the right to stand tall and that nobody can ride a back that isn't bent.

—Dorothy Cotton

Chapter 6
THE OBLIGATION TO SERVE
SHIRLEY CHISHOLM

—✂—

Service is the rent you pay for room on this earth.

—Shirley Chisholm

Growing up in Barbados and also in New York City, Shirley Chisholm earned a graduate degree from Columbia University in 1952. She was elected into Congress in 1968 and was the first African-American woman seated in the House of Representatives in 1969. And, in 1972, she became a candidate for the Presidency of the United States. In announcing her candidacy, Shirley Chisholm stated,

I stand before you today as a candidate for the Democratic nomination for the Presidency of the United States. I am not the candidate of black America, although I am black and proud. I am not the candidate of the women's movement of this country, although I am a woman, and I am equally proud of that. I am not the candidate of any political bosses or special interests. I am the candidate of the people.

As an opponent of the Vietnam War and a proponent of education and child welfare, she received only about 9% of the vote at the Democratic national convention. Shirley Chisholm was, and is, a woman who understands that in a society such as ours, service isn't a luxury; it is a necessity. May the rest of us plan our lives—and serve our neighbors—accordingly.

*A nation is formed by the willingness of each
of us to share in the responsibility for upholding the
common good.*

—Barbara Jordan

*Service is as much a part of my upbringing as eating
breakfast and going to school.*

—Marian Wright Edelman

*You don't need a college degree to serve. You don't
have to make your subject and verb agree to serve.
You don't have to know about Plato and Aristotle
to serve. You only need a heart full of grace and a
soul generated by love.*

—Johnetta B. Cole

Invest in a Human Soul.
Who Knows?
It Might be a Diamond
in the Rough.

—Mary McLeod Bethune

Talk without effort is nothing.

—Maria W. Stewart

You really can change the world if you care enough.

—Marian Wright Edelman

We must learn to deal with people positively and on an individual basis.

—Mary McLeod Bethune

Service is the purpose of life. In that context, you're not obligated to win. You're obligated to keep trying, to keep doing the best you can every day.

—Marian Wright Edelman

When do any of us do enough?

—Barbara Jordan

Everybody wants to do something to help, but nobody wants to be first.

—Pearl Bailey

When you find a man who has lost his way, you don't make fun of him and scorn him and leave him there. You show him the way. If you don't do that, you just prove that you're sort of lost yourself.

—*Zora Neale Hurston*

Enter school to learn; depart to serve.

—*Mary McLeod Bethune*

The cause of freedom is not the cause of a race or a sect, a party or a class; it is the cause of human kind, the very birthright of humanity.

—*Anna Julia Cooper*

*Our children must never lose their zeal for building
a better world.*

—Mary McLeod Bethune

*That's what being young is all about. You have the
courage and the daring to think that you can make
a difference. You're not prone to measure your energies
in time. You're not likely to live by equations.*

—Ruby Dee

*Motherhood is a profession by itself, just like school
teaching and lecturing.*

—Ida B. Wells

My parents were always philosophizing about how to bring about change. To me, people who didn't try to make the world a better place were strange.

—Carol Mosley-Braun

Our responsibility is to carry our generation one step forward.

—Mary McLeod Bethune

If you don't like the way the world is, you change it. You have an obligation to change it. You just do it one step at a time.

—Marian Wright Edelman

Chapter 7
GIVING THE PERFORMANCE
OF YOUR LIFE
ARETHA FRANKLIN
—⚡—

I put all my emotions into my music because that's what music is all about.

—*Aretha Franklin*

An incredibly powerful voice made this preacher's daughter from Detroit a musical icon. One poll even named her the greatest female artist in rock and roll history. She's Aretha Franklin, a down-to-earth star who attributed much of her success to the honest approach she brings to her craft. She said, "Great work and great music are the result of creative honesty."

Aretha Franklin is right: a great performance is an honest performance, but you don't have to have musical talent to give a good performance. Whether you are skilled in the areas of communication, management, or simply being a good friend, you can give a great performance when it's your time to shine. So today, as you step up on your stage, whether at work, home, or school, remember Aretha's success secret: do your work honestly, creatively, and diligently. When you do, your audience will smile, and so, too, will you.

You cannot fool an audience.

—Marian Anderson

Ego is a killer. Humility is probably the greatest power that one can study, to understand that you didn't create anything. God created it all.

—Melba Moore

A song has to become part of you. It's something in you that you'll have for the rest of your life.

—Martha Reeves

I don't wait for "moods." You accomplish nothing if you do that. You've got to get down to earth and go to work.

—Pearl Bailey

When I'm up on stage, it's my job to love the audience and share the gift God gave me.

—Pearl Bailey

The day I no longer go on stage will be the day I die.

—Josephine Baker

I don't sing my songs. I act them.

        —Tina Turner

The whole basis for my singing is feeling. Unless I feel something, I can't sing.

        —Billie Holiday

Sure I have a few aches and pains, but when I'm up on that stage, nothing hurts.

        —Pearl Bailey

When you look in the mirror, know who's looking back at you. When you know your strengths and recognize your weaknesses, you can create art.

—Debbie Allen

One needs occasionally to stand aside from the hum and rush of human interests and passions to hear the voices of God.

—Anna Julia Cooper

It's a joy to perform, and I want the audience to feel that joy.

—Pearl Bailey

I express myself through my music. I always have, and I always will.

—Marian Anderson

Seek to be an artist. Cease to be a drudge!

—Mary McLeod Bethune

My goal is to perform in such a way that someone in the audience leaves feeling a little better than when he came.

—Marian Anderson

If you feel a song, you can bet the audience will feel it, too.

—Billie Holiday

Chapter 8
OVERCOMING ADVERSITY, STRUGGLING FOR FREEDOM
LENA HORNE

—⋙—

As we live, we can either bloom or wilt. It's a personal choice.

—*Lena Horne*

In the 1940s, actresses of African-American descent were relegated to bit parts. The movies, it seemed, weren't ready for someone like Lena Horne. But Lena was ready for them. She parlayed a ton of talent and beauty into a career as a leading lady, something that, in those days, was unheard of for a woman of color. In looking back on her career, Lena was philosophical. She said, "The size of your burden is never as important as the way you carry it." Lena overcame this adversity and in doing so, enabled others to follow in her path, paving the way for future generations of actresses to become more readily accepted, widely admired, and highly sucessful.

The next time you face a heavy burden, remember that there is a good way and a bad way to carry every load. The best way is to keep working, keep believing, and never give in to discouragement. Because, as Lena Horne correctly observed, no load is too heavy if you discover the right way to carry it.

Laws will not eliminate prejudice from the hearts of human beings. But that is no reason to allow prejudice to continue to be enshrined in our laws to perpetuate injustice through inaction.

—*Shirley Chisholm*

Never work just for money or for power. They won't save your soul or help you sleep at night.

—*Marian Wright Edelman*

You may encounter many defeats, but you must not be defeated. In fact, it may be necessary to encounter the defeats, so you can know who you are, what you can rise from, and how you can still come out of it.

—*Maya Angelou*

In every crisis there is a message. Crises are nature's way of forcing change—breaking down old structures, shaking loose negative habits so something new and better can take their place.

—Susan L. Taylor

To struggle and battle and overcome and absolutely defeat every force designed against us is the only way to achieve.

—Nannie Burroughs

If these broken utterances can in any way help to a clearer vision and a truer pulse-beat in studying the Nation's Problem, this Voice by a Black Woman of the South will not have been raised in vain.

—Anna Julia Cooper

IT SEEMS ALMOST
PARADOXICAL, BUT NEVER
THE LESS TRUE, OF THE
HISTORY OF WOMEN AND
THE HISTORY OF NEGROES
ARE IN THE ESSENTIAL
FEATURES OF THEIR
STRUGGLE FOR STATUS,
QUITE PARALLEL.

—Mary Mc Leod Bethune

Of my two "handicaps," being female put many more obstacles in my path than being black.

—Shirley Chisholm

If our people are to fight their way out of bondage, we must arm them with the sword and the shield and the buckler of pride—belief in themselves and their possibilities based on a sure knowledge of the past.

—Mary McLeod Bethune

When we feel like the prey, a victim of evil pursuit, it's time for us to pray and take action against our predator.

—Seita Ann Jakes

*The struggle is much different now because racism
is more entrenched and complicated.*

—Angela Davis

*We need men and women whose hearts are the
homes of high and lofty enthusiasm and a noble
devotion to the cause of emancipation, who are ready
and willing to lay time, talent, and money on the
altar of universal freedom.*

—Frances Ellen Watkins Harper

*If people could make it in the darkness of slavery,
there is no excuse for us in the light of today's
alleged freedom.*

—Marva Collins

Liberation means you don't have to be silenced.

—Toni Morrison

We have to stop killing ourselves to solve our problems. The essence of nonviolence is love.

—*Dorothy Cotton*

Freedom was something internal. The outside signs were just signs and symbols of the man inside. All you do was to give the opportunity for freedom and the man himself must make his own emancipation.

—*Zora Neale Hurston*

A first generation American has as much claim to the legacy of Washington, Jefferson and Lincoln as those who can trace their roots to the Mayflower.

—*Condoleezza Rice*

I BELIEVE WE ARE HERE
ON THE PLANET EARTH
TO LIVE, GROW UP, AND
DO WHAT WE CAN
TO MAKE THIS WORLD
A BETTER PLACE
FOR ALL PEOPLE
TO ENJOY FREEDOM.

—Rosa Parks

IF FOLK CAN LEARN
TO BE RACIST,
THEN THEY CAN LEARN
TO BE ANTI-RACIST.

—Johnetta B. Cole

When Jesus Christ asked little children to come to him, he didn't say only rich children, or white children, or children with two-parent families, or children who didn't have a mental or physical handicap. He said, "Let all children come unto me."

—*Marian Wright Edelman*

The black woman has deep wells of spiritual strength.

—*Margaret Walker*

I have heard their groans and sighs, and seen their tears, and I would give every drop of blood in my veins to free them.

—*Harriet Tubman*

God is just. When he created man, he made him in his image and never intended one should misuse the other. All men are born free and equal in his sight.

　　　　　　　　　　—Susie King Taylor

I would fight for my liberty so long as my strength lasted, and if the time came for me to go, the Lord would let them take me.

　　　　　　　　　　—Harriet Tubman

If you and I don't build a bridge back, throw out some strong lifelines to our children, youth and families whom poverty, unemployment are engulfing, they're going to drown, pull many of us down with them, and undermine the future our forbears dreamed, struggled, and died for.

　　　　　　　　　　—Marian Wright Edelman

It is of no use for us to sit with hands folded, hanging our heads, lamenting our wretched condition; but let us make a mighty effort, and arise. And if no one will promote or respect us, let us promote and respect ourselves.

—Maria W. Stewart

I know we have made some progress over the years, but I know we also have to continue. We can't be too satisfied because we'll become complacent.

—Rosa Parks

Every man has his place in the world, but no man has the right to designate that place.

—Pearl Bailey

Nonviolence is…a spiritual discipline that requires a great deal of strength, growth, and purging of the self so that one can overcome almost any obstacle for the good of all without being concerned about one's own welfare.

—Coretta Scott King

*You have sung and prayed about dying and
forgiving your enemies and of feeling sure that
you're going to the New Jerusalem because your
God knows you're innocent. But, why don't
you pray to live and ask to be freed? The God
you serve is the God of Paul and Silas who opened
their prison gates. You ought to believe that he will
open your prison, too.*

—*Ida B. Wells*

*All the nations are crying out for liberty and
equality. Away, away with tyranny and oppression!*

—*Maria W. Stewart*

*On my underground railroad I never ran my train
off the track. And I never lost a passenger.*

—*Harriet Tubman*

We can't give up, we have got to continue…
We are not here to hold a position or to be head of
this, or that, or one of the other; we are here to mass
our power and our thinking and our souls to see
what we can do to make it better for that mass that
can't speak out there.

—Mary McLeod Bethune

I'm always making a comeback, but nobody ever tells
me where I've been.

—Billie Holiday

Sometimes I feel discriminated against, but it does
not make me angry. It merely astonishes me. How
can anyone deny themselves the pleasure of my
company? It's beyond me.

—Zora Neale Hurston

THE MOST
REWARDING FREEDOM
IS FREEDOM OF
THE MIND.

—*Amy Garvey*

Chapter 9
THE POWER OF LOVE
WILMA RUDOLPH

—◦◦◦—

We didn't look at it as being poor because you don't know that you're poor until you actually get out into the world. The love and the family support overshadowed our being poor.

—*Wilma Rudolph*

She was the twentieth of twenty-two children. As a child, she contracted polio and was forced to wear a brace to help her walk. But amazingly, just five years after taking that brace off her left leg, this determined sprinter won a bronze medal at the 1956 Olympics. Then four years later, in Rome, Wilma Rudolph became the first woman to win three gold medals in a single Olympic Games.

Although Wilma Rudolph grew up in poverty, her family was rich in love and support. And as we consider a well-lived life like Wilma's, we come to understand the genuine love—love that enriches and endures—is the greatest wealth of all.

Love is an element of principle that can stimulate the emotions and can cause one to be loyal.

—Rachel Hargrove Moore

Love wins when everything else will fail.

—Fanny Jackson Coppin

Loving your neighbor means being interracial, inter-religious, and international.

—Mary McLeod Bethune

Most of us love from our need to love, not because we find someone deserving.

—Nikki Giovanni

WHAT THE WORLD
REALLY NEEDS IS
MORE LOVE AND LESS
PAPERWORK.

—*Pearl Bailey*

*For in every human Breast, God has implanted
a Principle, which we call Love of Freedom; it is
impatient of Oppression, and pants for Deliverance.*

—*Phillis Wheatley*

*Life is a short walk from the cradle to the grave
and it behooves us to be kind to one another along
the way.*

—*Alice Childress*

You lose a lot of time hating people.

—*Marian Anderson*

Love, I find, is like singing. Everybody can do enough to satisfy themselves, though it may not impress the neighbors as being very much.

—*Zora Neale Hurston*

Thin love ain't love at all.

—*Toni Morrison*

Love is like playing checkers. You have to know which man to move.

—*Moms Mabley*

God is longing to love you.

　　　　　　　　　　—Tonya Bolden

*I have learned that the more we understand
how very much God loves us, and the more we
comprehend the grace He has demonstrated toward
us, the more humble we become.*

　　　　　　　　　　—Seita Ann Jakes

Love makes your soul crawl out of its hiding place.

　　　　　　　　　　—Zora Neale Hurston

Love stretches your heart and makes you big inside.

—Margaret Walker

I used to be very cold. When you are cold you miss passion in your life. I went for years just like ice. I was killing myself. I was not loving back.

—Lena Horne

WHEN ONE IS TOO OLD
FOR LOVE, ONE FINDS
GREAT COMFORT
IN GOOD DINNERS.

—*Zora Neale Hurston*

Chapter 10
EDUCATION, WISDOM, AND TRUTH
SOJOURNER TRUTH

Truth burns up error.   —*Sojourner Truth*

Isabella Bomefree (later spelled Baumfree) was born into slavery in 1797. Isabella was sold four times—the final time to a man named Van Wagener who gave Isabella and her daughter Sophia their freedom.

In 1843, Isabella experienced a spiritual transformation that caused her to change her name to Sojourner Truth. She then dedicated the rest of her life to the battle against slavery, oppression, and the terrible inequalities of her day.

Sojourner Truth became a powerful voice against the evils of 19th Century America. And when she published her autobiography, *The Narrative of Sojourner Truth: A Northern Slave,* in 1850, American readers took note.

Sojourner was a courageous woman who understood the power of words, the power of education, and the power of truth.

Today's population of descendents of slaves is testimony to the tenacity, foresight, and wisdom of millions of black women.

—Johnetta B. Cole

Follow your instincts. That is where true wisdom manifests itself.

—Oprah Winfrey

You never find yourself until you face the truth.

—Pearl Bailey

The essence of teaching is to make learning contagious, to have one idea spark another.

—Marva Collins

Most people know that facing the truth brings about healing and growth. When is America going to face its historical and current racial realities so it can be what it says it is?

—Camille Cosby

Threats cannot suppress the truth.

—Ida B. Wells

No person has the right to rain on your dreams.

—Marian Wright Edelman

The Lord will preserve me without weapons.
I feel safe even in the midst of my enemies, for the truth is all-powerful and will prevail.

—Sojourner Truth

Education empowers you; it places you in a position to verbally challenge people who are giving you a whole lot of nonsense.

—Camille Cosby

Education is the jewel casting brilliance into the future.

—Mari Evans

We do not have a money problem in America. We have a values and priorities problem.

—Marian Wright Edelman

Education remains the key to both economic and political empowerment.

—Barbara Jordan

Education is a precondition to survival in America today.

—Marian Wright Edelman

Good grades mean good dollars.

—Anita Baker

*When someone is taught the joy of learning,
it becomes a life-long process that never stops, a
process that creates a logical individual. That is the
challenge and the joy of teaching.*

—*Marva Collins*

*For every one of us who succeeds, it's because there's
somebody there to show us the way.*

—*Oprah Winfrey*

To Secure the Blessings
of Liberty, We Must
Secure the Blessings
of Learning.

— *Mary Futrell*

Education is for improving the lives of others and for leaving your community and world better than you found it.

—Marian Wright Edelman

Perhaps we should remind ourselves that the ultimate purpose of education is not to know but to act.

—Johnetta B. Cole

Through the children of today, we believe we can build the foundation of the next generation upon such a rock of morality, intelligence, and strength, that the floods of prescription, prejudice, and persecution may descend upon it in torrents and yet it will not be moved.

—Mary Church Terrell

A cynical young person is almost the saddest sight to see, because it means that he or she has gone from knowing nothing to believing nothing.

—Maya Angelou

Let there be light—two kinds of light: to light the outside world, and to light the world within the soul. Each generation with its own lamp gave out the lamp of learning and education.

—Mary McLeod Bethune

Never forget the struggles and the sacrifices of the generations of people who came before you— people who struggled and made possible the limitless opportunities that you now enjoy.

—Condoleezza Rice

Take charge. Ignorance is no longer a valid excuse. Empower yourself.

> —*Anita Baker*

Trying to grow up hurts. You make mistakes. You try to learn from them, and when you don't, it hurts even more.

> —*Aretha Franklin*

I am a woman in process. I'm just trying like everybody else. I try to take every conflict, every experience, and learn from it. Life is never dull.

> —*Oprah Winfrey*

You don't make progress by standing on the sidelines, whimpering and complaining. You make progress by implementing ideas.

> —*Shirley Chisholm*

Chapter 11
FAMILY AND FRIENDS
BESSIE & SADIE DELANEY
—⚏—

If Sadie is molasses, then I'm vinegar. Sadie is sugar and I'm spice…but we were best friends from Day One.

—Bessie Delaney

They were sisters and they were best friends. They were the incomparable centenarians, the Delaney sisters. Their father was born a slave and through their long lives, they witnessed incredible changes not only in race relations, but also in the American way of life.

When Bessie and Sadie Delaney published their memoirs in 1993, American readers rejoiced at the wit and wisdom of two women who had shared a hundred years together. Bessie Delaney, who lived to be 104 years young, was only the second African-American woman to be licensed to practice dentistry in New York. Sadie, who lived to be 109 years young, was the first black woman to teach domestic science in a New York high school. Both women were opinionated, insightful, and enthused about life.

The Delaney sisters understood the importance of family and the importance of friendship. And they both understood (from personal experience) that a beloved family member and a best friend are oftentimes one and the same.

*A friend gathers all the pieces and gives them back
in the right order.*

　　　　　　　　—Toni Morrison

*Being a friend means mastering the art of timing.
There is a time for silence. A time to let go and allow
people to hurl themselves into their own history.
And a time to pick up the pieces when it's all over.*

　　　　　　　　—Gloria Naylor

*Is there any solace more comforting than the arms
of a sister?*

　　　　　　　　—Alice Walker

A PERSON WITHOUT
FRIENDS MIGHT AS WELL
BE DEAD.

—Billie Holiday

COMMON DANGER

MAKES COMMON FRIENDS.

—Zora Neale Hurston

Woman, if the soul of the nation is to be saved,
I believe that you must become its soul.

—Coretta Scott King

We are a positively unique people.
Breathtaking people. Anything we do, we do big!

—Leontyne Price

A sister can be seen as someone who is both
ourselves and very much not ourselves—a special
kind of double.

—Toni Morrison

Home is where I know true peace and love.

—Anita Baker

*Momma was home. She was the most totally
human, human being that I have ever known;
and so very beautiful. She was the lighthouse
of her community. Within our home, she was an
abundance of love, discipline, fun, affection, strength,
tenderness, encouragement, understanding,
inspiration, and support.*

—Leontyne Price

A child is raised by the village.

—African Proverb

I can make something out of the children...
They have the essence of greatness in them.

—Zora Neale Hurston

NO PEOPLE NEED
EVER DESPAIR WHOSE
WOMEN ARE FULLY AROUSED
TO THE DUTIES WHICH
REST UPON THEM AND ARE
WILLING TO SHOULDER
RESPONSIBILITIES WHICH
THEY ALONE CAN
SUCCESSFULLY ASSUME.

—*Mary Church Terrell*

Oh ye mothers, what a responsibility rests on you! You have souls committed to your charge, and God will require a strict account of you.

—Maria W. Stewart

My mother taught me that nothing is gained without hardships or determination, and I attribute whatever success I may have had to her. I call her every day.

—Dorothy Dandridge

No race can afford to neglect the enlightenment of its mothers.

—Frances Ellen Watkins Harper

BLACK WOMEN
HAVE THE HABIT
OF SURVIVAL.

— *Lena Horne*

*I thank God for my grandmother who stood
on the word of God and lived with the spirit of
courage and grace.*

—*Maya Angelou*

*Your relationships with people begin in the
home, where you learn values. It's the responsibility
of the family.*

—*Melba Moore*

*You leave home to seek your fortune and when you
get it you go home and share it with your family.*

—*Anita Baker*

You can have the number-one album,
number-one-selling automobile, or whatever, but
if you don't have somebody to run home to and
jump up and down about it, then it's really empty.

—*Anita Baker*

Home is where you learn values. It's the responsibility
of the family.

—*Melba Moore*

Chapter 12
HAPPINESS
ZORA NEALE HURSTON

—⚏—

Happiness is nothing but everyday living seen through a veil.

—*Zora Neale Hurston*

Zora Neale Hurston graduated from Barnard College in 1928 and wrote about American folklore. She became the most widely read black woman in America, but was later abandoned by the publishing world. She died, largely forgotten, and was buried in a pauper's grave. But thankfully, the works of Zora Neale Hurston were rediscovered, and are once again in print and widely read.

Hurston observed that the secret to happiness lies in your perception of it. Aim to be an optimist and find something good in everything. So if you'd like to squeeze a little more enjoyment out of your day, don't look far out on the horizon; look for happiness in your daily life. If you don't find happiness close to home, you're unlikely to find it anywhere else.

I'm fulfilled in what I do. I never thought that a lot of money or fine clothes—the finer things of life— would make you happy. My concept of happiness is to be filled in a spiritual sense.

—Coretta Scott King

Being happy is not the only happiness.

—Alice Walker

If we stay with the Lord, enduring to the end of His great plan for us, we will enjoy the rest that results from living in the kingdom of God.

—Seita Ann Jakes

*I've had tragedy, but I have had lots of joy
and triumph.*

—*Coretta Scott King*

*God's love is unconditional, meaning He always
loves you, not just when you do something right.*

—*Seita Ann Jakes*

Each day, look for a kernel of excitement.

—*Barbara Jordan*

*People make a mistake in believing they're going
to be in paradise if they have more money.*

—*Mahalia Jackson*

Don't bring negatives to my door.

—*Maya Angelou*

Whatever you choose to do, you have one other obligation, and that is to yourself. Do it with passion. If you've not yet found your passion, keep searching. You never know when it will find you.

—*Condoleezza Rice*

Satisfaction is having only enough, but happiness is having enough to give to someone else.

—*Alice Hargrove Cutts*

Chapter 13
YOUR THOUGHTS
AND YOUR LIFE
LEONTYNE PRICE

—⚏—

If you're not feeling good about you, what you're wearing outside doesn't mean a thing.

—Leontyne Price

In 1927, Mary Violet Leontine Price was born in Laurel, Mississippi, the very heart of the segregated South. At an early age, she demonstrated remarkable musical talent. At the age of sixteen, Leontine sang her first formal recital, and soon she was off to college in Ohio. From there, the talented Miss Price enrolled in the Juilliard School of Music in New York. It was there that she changed the spelling of her name to Leontyne.

By the mid 1950s, Leontyne Price had propelled herself to the pinnacle of the world of opera. She toured extensively and made numerous appearances on national television. Leontyne's philosophy was simple; she said "Be Black, shine, aim high." With that positive attitude— and a heaping helping of talent—Miss Price aimed high and hit the mark. Because she had positive thoughts about her life and her aspirations, she never lost track of her goals. She rightly states that you have to have self-esteem and be convinced in your own abilities before you can convince anyone else.

If you want to accomplish the goals of your life, you have to begin with the Spirit.

—Oprah Winfrey

When you dream, you dialogue with aspects of yourself that normally are not with you in the daytime and you discover that you know a great deal more than you thought you did.

—Toni Cade Bambara

Whatever I'm doing, I don't think in terms of tomorrow. I try to live in the present moment.

—Anita Baker

The shortness of time, the certainty of death, and the instability of all things here to induce me to turn my thoughts from earth to heaven.

—Maria W. Stewart

I'm sick and tired of being sick and tired.

—Fanny Lou Hamer

I don't want others outside our community to define us, because they are doing a horrible job of it.

—Camille Cosby

Everybody has some special road of thought along which they travel when they are alone to themselves. And this road of thought is what makes every man what he is.

—Zora Neale Hurston

Be very careful what thoughts you put into your mind. For good or bad, they will boomerang right back to you.

—Beatryce Nivens

Forgiveness is nothing compared to forgetting.

—Bessie Delaney

When people made up their minds that they wanted to be free and took action, then there was change.

—Rosa Parks

My eyes and my mind keep taking me where my old legs can't keep up.

—Zora Neale Hurston

The need to change can bulldoze a road down the center of the mind.

— *Maya Angelou*

Intellect and brains and academics are fine, but we also have a heart and soul. It's okay to use all aspects of ourselves.

— *Dorothy Cotton*

If you haven't got pride, you can't show it. If you've got it, you can't hide it.

— *Zora Neale Hurston*

I thought I could change the world. It took me a hundred years to figure out I can't change the world. I can only change Bessie. And honey, that ain't easy either.

　　　　　　　　—Bessie Delaney

We have a powerful potential in our young people, and we must have the courage to change old ideas and practices so that we may direct their power toward good ends.

　　　　　　　—Mary McLeod Bethune

At present, our country needs women's idealism and determination, perhaps more in politics than anywhere else.

　　　　　　　　—Shirley Chisholm

Racial pride and self-dignity were emphasized in my family and community.

　　　　　　　　　—Rosa Parks

Chapter 14
THE COURAGE TO DREAM
MARY MCLEOD BETHUNE

—ᴧᴧ—

Most people think I'm a dreamer. And that's fine with me.
Through dreams many things come true.

—Mary McLeod Bethune

Mary McLeod Bethune was born in Mayesville, South Carolina. Her parents were former slaves. She had a tiny school and a very big dream: equal educational opportunities for African-Americans. In the beginning, she operated a one-room schoolhouse—on a shoestring—but she never lost sight of her goal. And she never lost hope.

Bethune promised that she would not rest until "there was not a single Negro boy or girl without a chance to prove his worth." Toward that end, she became president of the National Association of Colored Women in 1924. Soon thereafter, she became a trusted advisor and a friend to Eleanor Roosevelt. And as if those accomplishments weren't enough, Mary built her little one-room school into a respected institution of higher learning that still bears her name: Bethune-Cookman College.

Mary McLeod Bethune, the daughter of former slaves and a woman with few opportunities and countless roadblocks, went on to become an advisor to U. S. presidents, a renowned American educator, and tireless worker for liberty and equality. She dreamed big dreams and then worked diligently to make those dreams come true.

*I know what it means to hold dreams and
aspirations when half your neighbors think you are
incapable of, or uninterested in, anything better.*

—Condoleezza Rice

*We need visions of larger things, visions for the
unfolding of worthwhile things.*

—Mary McLeod Bethune

*You don't always reach a dream in the way
you first see it. When you get there, it's a different
dream, but it's still a dream.*

—Tina Turner

THE DREAM IS REAL,
MY FRIENDS.
THE FAILURE TO
MAKE IT WORK
IS THE UNREALITY.

—*Toni Cade Bambara*

We must aspire to be. And for all the things we are not, God will give us credit for trying.

—Nannie Burroughs

I always wanted to be somebody. If I made it, it's half because I was game enough to take a lot of punishment along the way and half because there were a lot of people who cared enough to help me.

—Althea Gibson

It isn't where you came from; it's where you're going that counts.

—Ella Fitzgerald

I had faith in a living God, faith in myself, and a desire to serve.

—Mary McLeod Bethune

Mama exhorted her children at every opportunity to "jump at de sun." We might not land on the sun, but at least we would get off the ground.

—Zora Neale Hurston

Never be limited by other people's limited imaginations. You can hear other people's wisdom, but you've got to re-evaluate the world for yourself.

—Mae Jemison

America's mission was and still is to take diversity and mold it into a coherent whole that would espouse virtues and values essential to the maintenance of civil order. There is nothing easy about that mission. But it is not mission impossible.

—Barbara Jordan

We have rarely worried about the odds or the obstacles before us, and we will not start worrying now. We will achieve our goals.

—Shirley Chisholm

Death cannot put the brakes on a big dream.

—Marva Collins

If one is lucky, a solitary fantasy can totally transform one million realities.

—Maya Angelou

'TWANT ME,
'TWAS THE LORD.
I ALWAYS TOLD HIM,
"I TRUST YOU. I DON'T
KNOW WHERE TO GO
OR WHAT TO DO,
BUT I EXPECT YOU
TO LEAD ME," AND
HE ALWAYS DID."

—*Harriet Tubman*

WE SPECIALIZE IN
DOING THE
WHOLLY IMPOSSIBLE.

—Nannie Burroughs

Chapter 15
All-Purpose Wisdom

—⚉—

The horizon leans forward, offering you space to place new steps of change.

—*Maya Angelou*

From musicians to educators and activists to athletes, African-American women are finally able to step into the spotlight and succeed in all areas of society. We must never forget the sacrifices of those strong women who came before us, opening countless doors of opportunity, breaking barriers, and stepping forward into uncertainty and adversity so that future generations could experience the best that life has to offer. But we must also never take our gifts for granted, and instead, continue to push forward, demand equality, educate ourselves and others, and strive to be the best women we can be.

After all, we owe much gratitude to our predecessors, and we owe ourselves nothing less than the highest heights we can possibly imagine. We are strong sisters, we are inspiring, we have depths of spirituality, personality, and practicality, and endless oceans of possibilities ahead of us.

Don't sit down and wait for the opportunities to come; you have to get up and make them.

—Madame C. J. Walker

Don't let anything stop you. There will be times when you will be disappointed, but you can't stop.

—Sadie T. M. Alexander

Don't wait for deliverers…I like that quotation, "Moses, my servant, is dead. Therefore, arise and go over Jordan." There are no deliverers. They're all dead. We must arise and go over Jordan. We can take the promised land.

—Nannie Burroughs

I would not exchange my color for all the wealth in the world.

—Mary McLeod Bethune

How Important it is
for Us to Recognize
and Celebrate Our
Heroes and She-roes!

—Maya Angelou

Seeking no favors because of our color or patronage because of our needs, we knock at the bar of justice and ask for an equal chance.

—*Mary Church Terrell*

Be careful, think about the effect of what you say. Your words should be constructive, bring people together, and not pull them apart.

—*Miriam Makeba*

Think like a queen. A queen is not afraid to fail. Failure is another stepping-stone to greatness.

—*Oprah Winfrey*

Before we even attempt to teach children, we want them to know that each of them is unique and very special. We want them to like themselves, to want to acheive and care about themselves.

—Marva Collins

If our children are to approve of themselves, they must see that we approve of ourselves.

—Maya Angelou

You can't eat everything you see.

—Bessie Delaney

Deal with yourself as an individual worthy of respect, and make everyone else deal with you in the same way.

—Nikki Giovanni

IF YOU ASK ME THE
SECRET TO LONGEVITY,
I WOULD TELL YOU THAT
YOU HAVE TO WORK AT
TAKING CARE OF YOUR
HEALTH. BUT, A LOT
OF IT IS ATTITUDE, TOO.
I AM ALIVE OUT OF SHEER
DETERMINATION, HONEY!

—*Bessie Delaney*

*Defeat should not be the source of discouragement,
but a stimulus to keep plotting.*

—*Shirley Chisholm*

*If you want to be successful, you don't have time
for bitterness.*

—*Tina Turner*

*To live is to suffer; to survive is to find some
meaning in the suffering.*

—*Roberta Flack*

The kind of beauty I want most is the hard-to-get kind that comes from within—strength, courage, dignity.

—Ruby Dee

I'll wrestle me up a future or die trying.

—Zora Neale Hurston

One thing is clear to me: We, as human beings, must be willing to accept people who are different from ourselves.

—Barbara Jordan

Our ancestors are an ever-widening circle of hope.

—*Toni Morrison*

The greatest gift is not being afraid to question.

—*Ruby Dee*

I constantly felt (as I suppose many an ambitious girl has felt) a thumping from within unanswered by any beckoning from without.

—*Anna Julia Cooper*

All my life I've worked with youth. I have begged for them and fought for them and lived for them and in them. My story is their story.

—Mary McLeod Bethune

Organize yourself inside. Teach your children the internals and the externals, rather than just the externals of clothing and money.

—Nannie Burroughs

I think it took having children for me to get everything in the right place.

—Tina Turner

*When I participated in the world of sports, we
stuck with the basics: determination, inspiration,
and hard work.*

—Wilma Rudolph

*When aroused, the American conscience is a powerful
force for reform.*

—Coretta Scott King

There was one or two things I had a right to, liberty or death. If I could not have one, I would have the other, for no man should take me alive. I should fight for my liberty as long as my strength lasted.

—*Harriet Tubman*

How can we create a harmonious society out of so many kinds of people? The key is tolerance.

—*Barbara Jordan*

BECAUSE TIME
HAS BEEN GOOD TO ME,
I TREAT IT WITH
GREAT RESPECT.

~ Lena Horne

You must learn to say no when something is not right for you.

—*Leontyne Price*

If you get there—to success that is, you will not have gotten there on your own.

—*Johnetta B. Cole*

Malcolm is gone and Martin is gone and it is up to all of us to nourish the hope they gave us.

—Lena Horne

A lot of people are waiting for Martin Luther King or Mahatma Gandhi to come back—but they are gone. We are it. It is up to us. It is up to you.

—Marian Wright Edelman

I DO NOT WEEP AT
THE WORLD—I AM TOO
BUSY SHARPENING
MY OYSTER KNIFE.

—Zora Neale Hurston

Sources

Sadie T. M. Alexander   *Lawyer and Activist (1898-1989)*

Debbie Allen   *Dancer, Actress, Choreographer*

Marian Anderson   *Singer*

Maya Angelou   *Poet, Author, Playwright, Actress*

Pearl Bailey   *Singer (1918-1990)*

Anita Baker   *Singer*

Josephine Baker   *Dancer, Entertainer (1906-1975)*

Toni Cade Bambara   *Writer (1939-1995)*

Mary Frances Berry   *Civil Right Activist*

Mary McLeod Bethune   *Educator (1875-1955)*

Tonya Bolden   *Author*

Julia Boyd   *Psychotherapist*

Ruth Brown   *Singer*

Nannie Burroughs   *American Educator, National Training School for Girls (1879-1961)*

Alice Childress   *Actress, Playwright (1920-1994)*

Shirley Chisholm   *First African-American Woman Elected to Congress, b. 1925*

Johnetta B. Cole   *Educator*

SOURCES

—៣—

Marva Collins	*Educator*
Anna Julia Cooper	*Educator, Writer, Feminist (1859-1964)*
Fanny Jackson Coppin	*Educator (1835-1912)*
Camille Cosby	*Philanthropist, Activist, Wife of Bill Cosby*
Dorothy Cotton	*Civil Rights Activist, Education Director for the Southern Christian Leadership Conference Under Martin Luther King, Jr. (b. 1931)*
Dorothy Dandridge	*Actress (d. 1965)*
Angela Davis	*Political Activist, Professor*
Ruby Dee	*Actress*
Bessie Delaney	*Author (1891-1995)*
Marian Wright Edelman	*Lawyer, Educator, Activist, Children's Advocate, Recipient of MacArthur Genius Award (b. 1939)*
Mari Evans	*Educator, Writer (b. 1923)*
Ella Fitzgerald	*American Singer*
Roberta Flack	*Singer*

Sources

—✺—

Aretha Franklin	*Singer*
Mary Futrell	*Educator*
Amy Garvey	*Civil Rights Activist, Businesswoman, First Wife of Marcus Garvey (1897-1969)*
Althea Gibson	*Tennis player*
Nikki Giovanni	*American poet*
Fanny Lou Hamer	*Civil Rights Activist (1917-1977)*
Frances Ellen Watkins Harper	*Author, Activist (1825-1911)*
Billie Holiday	*Singer (1915-1959)*
Lena Horne	*Singer (b. 1917)*
Zora Neale Hurston	*Author (1891-1960)*
Mahalia Jackson	*Singer (1911-1972)*
Seita Ann Jakes	*Writer, Wife of T. D. Jakes*
Mae Jemison	*Astronaut*
Barbara Jordan	*Politician, Educator (1936-1996)*
Florence Griffith Joyner	*Track and Field Star*
Coretta Scott King	*Civil Rights Activist, Wife of Martin Luther King, Jr.*

Sources

—∿—

Eartha Kitt	*Actress*
Patti LaBelle	*Singer*
Audre Lorde	*Poet, Activist*
Moms Mabley	*Comedienne*
Miriam Makeba	*South-African-born Entertainer*
Melba Moore	*Singer, Philanthropist*
Toni Morrison	*Writer, Nobel Laureate*
Carol Mosley-Braun	*First African-American Woman Elected to Senate*
Gloria Naylor	*Novelist (b. 1950)*
Beatryce Nivens	*Speaker, Author*
Rosa Parks	*Civil Rights Activist (b. 1913)*
Leontyne Price	*Singer (b. 1927)*
Martha Reeves	*Singer*
Condoleezza Rice	*National Security Advisor, Educator*
Wilma Rudolph	*Track and Field Star (1940-1994)*
Maria W. Stewart	*Political Writer (1803-1879)*
Susie King Taylor	*Former Slave and Army Nurse (1856-1915)*

Sources

Susan L. Taylor	*Editor, Speaker, Spokeswoman*
Mary Church Terrell	*Civil Right Activist, Feminist (1863-1954)*
Sojourner Truth	*Social Activist (1797-1883)*
Harriet Tubman	*Abolitionist (1820-1913)*
Tina Turner	*Singer*
Cicely Tyson	*Actress*
Alice Walker	*Author*
Margaret Walker	*Educator, Poet (1915-1998)*
Ethel Waters	*Singer, Actress (1896-1977)*
Maxine Waters	*Singer, Actress (1896-1977)*
Ida B. Wells	*Activist, Writer, Reformer (1862-1931)*
Phillis Wheatley	*America's First African-American Poet, Former Slave (1753-1784)*
Oprah Winfrey	*Television Personality*